THAR'S "GOLD"WINGS, HARLEYS AND OTHER MOTORCYCLES IN THEM THAR HILLS

ERIC WIEBERG

DEDICATION

This book is dedicated first and foremost to my loving wife Debra, who has stood by me through the past 5 years as I have built the dream of www.northgeorgiamotorcycles.com into more than just a hobby. She has devoted herself to helping me build not only a place on the web, but a physical riding group that meets and rides year around in (on more than one occasion) rain, snow & sleet. This group meets monthly and this book shares some of the rides and fun times that we have had over 5 years!

Secondly, I want to dedicate this book to my father & mother, Howard & Lana Wieberg and my son, Jon Wieberg for the countless time and resources which they have provided that have enabled me to spend the time building such a group and to write this book.

Finally, I would like Craig & Nancy Rutledge to share in the dedication of this book, as they have stood by me from the beginning days and were part of our original group of riders. It has been my privilege to see Craig go from a determined rider of a Piaggio MP3 250cc 3-wheeled Scooter to an experienced rider of a Triumph Rocket 2300cc Motorcycle. Craig and Nancy have always been there with smiles on their faces, willing to help in any way they could, whether it be to lead a ride, plan a ride, find a good restaurant (Craig seems to do a great job at this - we think he is really a hobbit in disguise, as he must eat at least 6 meals a day and remains as skinny as a rail!), or just be there for encouragement!

To all, I just want to say a sincere heart felt "Thank You". I could not have done this without any one of you!

CONTENTS

ACKNOWLEDGMENTS

I would like to acknowledge just a few people that have helped me over the past year in bringing this book to a reality. First and foremost, I need to recognize my father, Howard Wieberg, for all of the countless hours that he has put in manning the retail shop while I was out calling on businesses. He has also put countless hours into editing and proofreading this book for me. Please don't crucify him if you find something that he has missed!

Secondly, I would like to thank my son, Jon, for the time that he has put in at the store, as well as for his article in chapter 2.

Thirdly, a special "thank you" to George Dangler and the staff at Union PowerSports in Blairsville, GA for the past 5 years of making sure that we always had the bikes that we needed. I do find it interesting that George kept finding ways to upgrade me until I wound up on a Honda Goldwing! I must say that without the Goldwing, I believe that it would have been next to impossible to travel 1.000 mile weeks, week in and week out last summer to visit so many businesses and lead so many rides!

Finally, to all of the business owners that have had the faith to believe in us both on the www.northgeorgiamotorcycles.com website and by supporting the writing of this book!

Thank YOU!

It's all about the Ride!

The chapters in this book are for your enjoyment about the ride to different locations, beginning from locations in North Georgia.

I have tried to keep the chapters short, but still give you enough information to encourage you to visit these locations!

I believe we live in an area of the country that has been hand crafted for motorcyclists of all kinds! We have everything from twisties and high mountains with the Blue Ridge Parkway and the Cherohala Skyway to the world famous Tail of the Dragon! We also have within our riding circle, simple back country roads with gentle rolling hills, such as the ride to Cloudland Canyon.

I have not covered all of these rides within this book, but rather, I have decided to save them for another volume.

THAR'S "GOLD"WINGS, HARLEYS AND OTHER MOTORCYCLES IN THEM THAR HILLS

1 NORTH GEORGIA – HOME SWEET HOME

As a boy growing up in upstate New York, I had always heard about Georgia. I could not wait until I had the chance to visit there; after all, the whole state was "swamps and gators"! This was what we had been told about Georgia from those traveling to Florida for their winter vacations every year, other than the fact that it came after "Pedro's South of the Border"!

Contrary to all of the rumors, after my wife and I married, I decided to continue my education and return to college in (you guessed it) Georgia. We packed our U-Haul truck and headed out in the middle of a driving snow storm for the Sunny, Warm South (or at least we thought). When we arrived in North Georgia, we discovered that they had temps like we had in New York; it was in the 20's and freezing cold! Within one week of moving here, we were greeted with 6" of snow. This was a far cry from the land of Swamps and Gators that I had been told about! The other thing that I noticed was that Georgia had mountains – it was beginning to look a lot like home, as we had just left the Adirondack Mountains of Upstate New York some 900 miles behind us.

Our move to Georgia in January 1982 landed us in a little town named Toccoa, located in Northeast Georgia on the South Carolina Border. From Toccoa, we would travel up Hwy 17 and pick up Hwy 441 and wind up in places like Clayton and Tallulah Gorge or Helen, Georgia. Little did I ever realize that some 30 years later the names of these towns would have such an impact on my life! I even used to go deer hunting in some little town named Ellijay, never expecting that this would be where I would someday wind up raising my son and making my home there.

Toccoa Falls on the campus of Toccoa Falls College

Upon leaving Toccoa, Debbie and I moved to the Metro Atlanta area in Stone Mountain, and eventually Lawrenceville. While we were living in Lawrenceville, our son Jon was born, and we watched him grow into a young child full of ambition. During this time, we took several family outings to the mountains and watched Jon just eat up his time there. In 1993, we bought property in Ellijay, figuring that one day we would build a cabin there. By 1995, we had spent so much time there (every chance we could get); that we decided it was time to move to the mountains!

We moved to Ellijay in 1995, where I opened a business, and our lives became rooted here. After living here for about 5 years, we decided that Georgia was not all about Swamps and Gators and we decide to buy a small horse farm here in the mountains. Life was good, my son was growing up in the country, I had recently picked up a motorcycle in trade for some work that I did for a guy, and we were really enjoying life in the mountains of North Georgia. Over the next several years, my wife and I watched as our son grew into a young man and became a very avid horseman, riding in competitions around the state and just enjoying life. We did not think life could get any better! We had made North Georgia "Home Sweet Home"!

Carter's Lake in Ellijay, GA

Life continued on as normal until we all got hit with the big surprise of gasoline prices jumping to $4.15 a gallon in 2008. Remember my mentioning in the previous paragraph that I had acquired a motorcycle in a trade? It was a 1983 Honda Shadow 500. I had grown up riding motorcycles, and Debbie and I even had one when we first got married in 1979, but we had taken about 17 years away from the hobby until I made the trade. I rode the Shadow on and off for a few years, but somehow it got parked and I didn't ride it for about 5 years while we were playing the horse game. In 2008, when the gas prices sky-rocketed, Debbie told me that if I wasn't going to ride the bike, she was going to get her license and ride. That statement has changed our lives forever!

July 4th weekend of 2008, we went to Canton, GA to order some parts for the 1983 Honda and while I was ordering parts, Debbie was looking at scooters. At the time, Cycle Nation had not yet purchased

Honda of Canton and their inventory was low. They were selling their last scooter to someone else, but I could tell where this was headed. After ordering the parts, we climbed into the car and headed to the Motions Motorcycle Dealer in Marietta to look at scooters. Long story short, I drove a 2008 Yamaha Morphus 250 cc Scooter home for Debbie that day. When we got home, she informed me that since I had ordered the parts for the 1983 Shadow, I could fix that up and ride it.

Debbie's 2008 Yamaha Morphus Scooter

Obviously, the more that I thought about this deal, it just was not right - I was the experienced rider, and I should have a new bike! So, when I went back to Canton to pick up the parts for the '83 Shadow, I came home with a new 2008 Honda Shadow 750 Aero.

What had I done? Remember that I said I had parked the '83 Shadow for about five years? During the time it was sitting there, my son Jon had turned old enough to get his license, and he wanted a motorcycle license. Being full of wisdom and knowledge, and like most dads, I told him that it was too dangerous! But, now - dear old mom & dad BOTH had motorcycles. Have you ever eaten crow????

Now I had to make a decision. Would I say "do as I say, not as I do" or would I help him in getting his license, too? Guess what? We all now ride!

Eric's 2008 Honda Shadow Aero 750

This now presented another dilemma for me. Debbie and I now had bikes to ride, but no one to share the joy of riding with. Owning a computer business and developing web sites for people, I decided that I could develop a website where people could simply post about their riding experiences in North Georgia, and that Debbie and I would probably get to meet a few of them and become riding buddies. Little did I know how much people were looking for a site like this, and all of a sudden it took off like wildfire. People starting using http://northgeorgiamotorcycles.com like crazy, and sure enough, before long, Larry from the Dalton area contacted me and said "Hey - can we meet up someplace and ride?"

I had started the website in October 2008. Larry and I rode together in December 2008, January and February 2009. In March 2009, I published on the website that we would ride along the Ocoee

River and stop at the site of the 1996 White Water Olympic events. We had five new riders join us for that ride; Craig Rutledge was one of those riders. Craig has been with me ever since, and this book is in part dedicated to Craig and Nancy for all of their help over the years! We have been riding on the third Saturday of every month except December since that time.

Over the period of the past five years, some exciting things have happened. My son, Jon, started by riding his mother's scooter, then successfully obtained his motorcycle license and has since purchased two motorcycles, a 2010 Kawasaki Ninja 250 which he later traded for a 2012 Kawasaki Ninja 650R. He has written a comical view of his first road trip to Florida on his mother's scooter. You find it reproduced for the 2nd chapter of this book. I have since upgraded my bike twice, once to a 2009 Honda VTX1300R and then to a 2012 Honda GL1800 Goldwing. My wife tells me that I can't upgrade anymore, I am at the top of the ladder! She has upgraded from the scooter to a 2009 Kawasaki Vulcan 500 LTD. These past five bikes that I have mentioned have all come from Union PowerSports in Blairsville, GA. I feel like we should own some stock in the company, but all George Dangler, owner, does is sit back and smile!

Eric's 2009 Honda VTX 1300R

2010 Kawasaki Ninja 250

Jon and his 2012 Kawasaki Ninja 650R

Debbie on her 2009 Kawasaki Vulcan 500 LTD

Eric on his 2012 Honda GL1800 Goldwing

The www.northgeorgiamotorcycles.com Website has been so successful that in October 2011, people using the website started requesting me to create a directory of motorcycle-friendly businesses in the North Georgia towns where the rides that we publish take place. I have started the directory on the website, and publish businesses in towns even if we haven't run a ride there, but it's a popular route.

A few of the businesses that are on the website and are very biker friendly have asked to be included in this book. They are listed here or with a full page ad throughout the book. Chapter 9 includes a full listing of the select businesses in this book that would appreciate your support

Ellijay, GA:

Cajun Depot Grill (Restaurant)
67 Depot Street Suite 101, Ellijay, GA 30540
706-276-1676

Panorama Orchards & Farm Market (Apple Orchard & Market)
Hwy 515 South
63 Talona Spur
Ellijay, GA 30540
706-276-3813

Walker's Fried Pies & BBQ (BBQ & Homemade Fried Pies)
2183 Georgia 52 East
Ellijay, GA 30536
(706) 635-1223

Southern Grace (Southern Country Charm Home Accents)
40 River St., Suite A
Ellijay, GA 30540
706-515-1090
706-515-1093

Whistle Tree Pottery (Beautiful Pottery for the Home)
10 North Main Street
Ellijay, GA 30540
706-698-1223

Fairmount, GA:

GMD Computrack Atlanta/Motorcycle Pro Care (Repair Shop)
106 S Ave
Fairmount, GA 30139
(706) 337-4114

Murphy, NC:

Best Western of Murphy
1522 Andrews Road
Murphy, NC 28906
828-837-3060

Thanks to all of you who use the website! We are currently running anywhere from the Number 1 Listing to the Number 5 Listing in all search engines for motorcycle rides in north Georgia.

You are the reason for this book and you have truly made North Georgia – Home Sweet Home!

Eric Wieberg

12

2 JON'S RIDE

In this chapter, I have chosen to reproduce my son Jon's article that is posted on our www.northgeorgiamotorcycles.com website. In this article, Jon recreates the first motorcycle adventure that he truly encountered.

Jon had so anxiously wanted his license in order to go for a trip to Florida by motorcycle that he braved rain and freezing cold temperatures to go take his road test just a few days before we left. I have learned that February can be more brutal than December and January, which we normally think of as the hard winter months. I was reminded of this once again this past weekend when we ran a ride for North Georgia Motorcycles and Born to Ride Magazine.

The following is the reprint of Jon's Article about his first long distance motorcycle ride. After having his learner's permit for 6 months, he went and got his license just a week prior to our leaving on this trip from Ellijay, GA to Panama City Beach, FL. When we left Ellijay, the temperature was 22 degrees and it remained cold for the next 400 miles!

Jon is 21 (now 25) and documented this description of his trip from a comical viewpoint. Enjoy!

The following is a vivid account of a trip from the small town of Ellijay, GA to the happenin' city of Panama City Beach. Some of the following may be unsuitable for minors due to the intensely graphic nature of the crash scene. If you start feeling dizzy or nauseous, please step away from the monitor and take a deep breath. It will be okay.

Our morning started out at roughly 7:00 AM (Eastern Time). Slowly we arose and got busy doing the things that people do when going on trips. This however, was to be no ordinary trip. That's right... this was a motorcycle road trip. Four hundred miles in one direction, and the temperature was below thirty. Yes, my children... it was Cold!

I spent the last few minutes of my warm life talking on messenger to a friend. I told them that the plan was to leave at 9:00 AM (Eastern Time). Slowly the clock counted down to that dreadful hour. Finally, at about 8:30 AM (Eastern Time), I shut down the computer. We were almost ready... However, somehow it took us nearly another hour to get out the door (after sweeping and doing those things that my dear mother deems necessary).

9:30 AM
We head out the driveway.
9:36 AM
We pull into the Gilmer County Bank parking lot, and readjust all our gear.
9:45 AM
We pull out of the bank parking lot, and hit the road for Florida!
9:51 AM
We stop again. My hands are freezing, and I have to change gloves.
9:54 AM
We hit the road again...
9:59 AM
We stop yet again. The vents on my helmet are pouring cold air in and hitting my forehead, making my brain and eyes ache.
10:02 AM
We're off yet again. The wind is bitter cold. Within minutes, all my vital body parts are shutting down. We're not going to make it.
10:17 AM
My father pulls off in Jasper, Ga. reconfirming my belief that there is a God. We stop for Starbucks coffee, and all is well with the world.
10:45 AM
We finally leave Starbucks, dear sweet Starbucks. We resolve to not stop until Canton.
11:05 AM
We make it to Canton and stop at Cycle Nation to buy better gloves.

11:30 AM

Time to hit the road again. It is decided that we're not stopping until the other side of Atlanta.

12:30 PM

Passing through downtown Atlanta.

12:58 PM

My balaclava and glasses are causing a bunch on my ear, causing it to hurt tremendously. I try to get dad's attention, to no avail.

1:15 PM (130 miles)

We finally pull off at an exit, looking for sustenance. We miss our turn and stop in a subdivision. Before dad can make me leave, I shut down the engine and yank off my helmet. My ear is mauled and bleeding... from the feel of it. It however, is just red and sore. After jogging around for a couple minutes to get feeling back in my legs, we decide to head back to our missed turn and get something to eat.

1:25 PM (Content advisory)

I gear back up... but I forgot to put on my glasses. I left them sitting on the "dash" of the bike. We start heading down the road, and as I round a corner they slip off the dash and clatter onto the road. My heart jumps into my chest, and my life flashes before my blind eyes. I quickly pulled into another subdivision and turned the bike around. Mom followed me, not knowing what was going on. I slowly drove back down the road, looking for them. I saw them and pointed it out to the car behind me, hoping they wouldn't hit them. Luckily, they didn't.

As I parked the bike and climbed off, dad pulled in. The car behind him swerved to go around. That's when I heard it. The sounds of ultimate doom. The bane of my drive to Florida. It was the demolishment of my glasses. I stared in horror as the next car hit it as well, and the lens went flying down the road. This was going to be a very long trip.

Though I have been told to never leave a man behind, I had to turn my back upon my dear friend.

Good bye, you will be sorely missed.

1:36 PM

We arrive at Blimpies for lunch.

2:04 PM

After eating a bag of chips and drinking a Pepsi, I pulled the bike around to get some gas. Dad does the same, at which point a man approaches us. Dad and he get talking, and it turns out that he is from the CMA (Christian Motorcyclist Association). After chatting a little, he prays for us, and we head on our way once more.

3:12 PM (180-190 miles)

Arrived in Columbus rest area. Met a couple riding Harleys, and chatted with them for a little while. Also talked to the grounds keeper at the rest area, who was very interested in mom's scooter. He asked lots of questions, and thought it was quite interesting.

3:45 PM

Left rest area.

5:02 PM

We stopped in the "hood" of Eufaula, Alabama for gasoline. Snickered at the signs on the door.

"No shirt — No shoes — Low pants — No service"

6:05 PM

Stopped in Dothan and scarfed down a big mac and coffee. Stomach ache ensued.

6:46 PM (85 miles to go)

Changed shield on helmet to clear (because it was dark), and hit the road again.

7:22 PM (44 miles to go)

Stopped for a while to warm up. Core body temperature had dropped significant amount. Disorientation setting in.

7:40 PM

Headed out again.

8:10 PM (21 miles to go)

Stopped again to warm up. Core body temperature getting quite low. Disorientation getting a little worrisome.

8:32 PM

Headed out once more.

9:04 PM

We arrived in the Panama City outskirts, and stopped for gas. I could not control my hands, and when I could feel them, they would have pain shoot through them.

9:16 PM
Headed out for the last 10 mile leg of our journey.
9:46 PM
We arrive at our destination!! Cold, weary, and sore.
10:00 PM
I take my first walk on the beach in three years. I call my friends to let them know I have arrived safe and sound. Only took twelve hours, when it was supposed to have only been about seven. Overall, it was a really good trip. A good bit colder than I was hoping for, but still a good one for my first long trip.

R.I.P.
Glasses…

Tips for the long distance biker:
Order hot drinks at stops. Ice is not your friend.
Get a mouth guard. Don't chew on your tongue.
Hug the engine of your following car, whenever you can.
If you don't have a car, hug the exhaust pipe on your bike.
It is interesting, the amount of heat one can glean from a street light
Don't worry about looking like a fool doing jumping-jacks in a parking lot. They'll never see you again.
Don't irritate the woman in the car behind you, even if she is your mother.
Downing a Big Mac in less than 30 seconds is not advisable, no matter how hungry you are.
If you wear glasses, get a nerd cord.

My son's first long distance trip - Part II - The Return!

There comes a time in every man's life that he starts to worry that he made a big mistake. Yes… it is true men, don't try to deny it. I have not come to that point in my life yet, but I was worried I had when I was driving home from Florida.

Now, you might be thinking, "Driving home from Florida? What's the big deal about that?" — Well, let me tell you. Yes, on this fateful couple of days, I was on a motorcycle, a four hundred mile journey to the northern section of Georgia. Luckily, I was not alone on this journey. My father was also riding his motorcycle, and my mother was in the car following us.

Yes, on this fateful day we got a late start out of Panama City Beach. We had stopped for breakfast, and took longer than we should have. Once we finished up there, we headed on our way. By this time, it was roughly eleven o'clock in the morning. Once we got on the road, it wasn't long before we stopped for the first time. There's a motorcycle shop on the outskirts of town that we had made a couple trips to, and we stopped one more time before we left.
Once we left there, about an hour later, we headed on for Columbus. We had decided that we would try to make it there before dark. We didn't make a whole lot of stops along the way. One or two bathroom breaks, and that was it. Sounds boring, yes?

On one of our bathroom stops, we noticed that the clouds ahead of us were getting really dark. We decided that we should get our rain suits on before we kept going. So we put our suits on, and I went back inside to get a quick drink. While I am waiting in line I hear the weather station come on, but I don't really think much about it. That is, until I hear the word.... Tornado. That's right. That was my thought when I heard it too.

We hit the road again, but going slower as the wind is starting to kick up a little bit. I can hear some of you thinking already, "Are you guys idiots?! There's a tornado out there!!". Well, to calm your thoughts for now, it wasn't where we were going. Just knowing it was out there was scary enough, though. — Where was I? Ah yes... We got a few miles down the road, and it started to rain. Not too bad, but enough to get annoying. For the most part, we didn't have many problems until we got right outside of Columbus right as it was turning dark.

A little advice if you're ever in Columbus on a motorcycle at night when it's raining: Don't.

You know how on some roads they have that patching material that they drizzle on the roads to make it "smoother"? Well, motorcycle tires do not like that stuff very well, when it's wet, doubly so. Well, in

Columbus… they practically paved with the stuff, at least, where the regular car tires go. So that left the middle of the road open for me to drive on. Guess where all the oil surfaces when it rains? Yeah, that's right. This left me with a two inch section of road to drive on, with a 4 inch tire. Remember… I am also fighting gusts of wind.

Meanwhile, it's grown dark and cold. I still have on my tinted face shield. It gets too dark to see, so I have to raise it. It's raining remember, and the rain is slapping into my face and stinging like a bunch of needles. Not to mention, I don't even have the protection of my glasses any more. I also still have on my summer gloves, so what's left of my hands is soaking wet and cold.
But what's this? — A beacon of hope in the ever growing darkness? A turn signal! I can see the light!

My father turns into a hotel parking lot. At last! Rest for my frozen epidermis! I climb off the motorcycle and prepare for the glorious heat that awaits me in the hotel room. Yesss… I can feel it no——
What do you mean no rooms?

Two hotels later, we finally find room. Even at a hundred dollars a night, it is worth it. I slowly peel off my layers of clothing, worrying that might skin might go with it, and stand in front of the heater. After a few minutes, my phone rings. I slowly reach into my pocket (fingers breaking off in the process) and pull out my phone. A familiar name! My friend Lauren is calling to check up on me. Man, she's awesome.
I open the phone and am greeted with, "Where have you been?" — Whoa… When did I get married? We talk for a while, and she tells me that she was driving in Atlanta traffic for 7 hours, and had been waiting to talk to me for nearly as long. We talked for a while, and finally got off the phone… I crash into bed, get out my computer, and talk to a few friends for a while. Meanwhile, the rain tries to take the building down.

The next morning, we awake to angry skies. On goes the weather channel, and it's not looking good. We decide we're going to make a break for it. We'll get an early start and beat it out. Mom packs up her stuff and heads for the car. As she is going to breakfast, the skies open up. God didn't renege on the whole flooding the earth thing, did he?

Alright, so we're not leaving for a little while. We'll just wait it out... uh-huh.

Knock knock.

Who is it? — There's no answer.

Who iiiis it? — There's still no answer.

— Wait, that's a Weird Al song. We weren't as fortunate.

Knock knock.

Who is it?

Housekeeping...

We open the door. They have a funny look on their face.

Yeeeah... We need you to get into the stairwell... There's a tornado headed this way.

Uh-huh... Well, this should be fun.

We headed to the stairwell, and packed in like sardines with the other poor hapless victims, and took pictures on our cell phones. After a while, the staff came around and handed out pillows. They told us that the tornado was fairly close and they would let us know of any updates. Great.

After a while, they came around and told us it was all clear to come out, but it was still raining very hard. We made an executive decision that we would need to stay another day, because we couldn't ride in the kind of weather that was being thrown at us. So, we paid and went back up to our room.

Fast forward a couple hours... Open the curtains, seeing if the rain has let up yet — Uhm. What's this? Sunshine? Blue sky? Get the dang car packed, we're blowing this joint.

We get all geared up, and head downstairs. After taking the covers off the bikes (which are full of water), we head on. How things can change in just a short period of time.

We had relatively no problem the rest of the way home. We drove about one hundred miles in twilight/dark, but that was about it.

Goodness, it felt so good to be home. Never thought my mattress would feel so good.

So, though I was starting to think that this may have been one of "those mistakes" in my life, it was surprisingly not all that bad. There were only a few memorable moments in my trip that I thought I was going to be hurt pretty badly, so all in all… a good trip.

Gosh, this post was too long.

Tips for the long distance biker:
Though you may look like a smurf, rain gear is your friend.
Tinted face shields are not conducive to night riding.
Work out a signal to let the other riders know when you need to use the bathroom. This can mean the difference between life and death.
When in doubt about needing to stay another night in a hotel, wait in the lobby.
Put on your warm gloves before you need them.
Get earplugs for long distance highway trips.

3 THE CHEROHALA SKYWAY

Probably one of the most requested rides that we have done over the years is the Cherohala Skyway, located between Robbinsville, NC and Tellico Plains, TN.

This ride is perhaps the one of the most beautiful rides on the Eastern Coast in the foothills of the Great Smokey Mountains and the Appalachian Mountain Range.

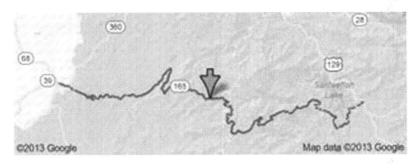

The Cherohala Skyway is a 43-mile National Scenic Byway that connects Tellico Plains, Tennessee, to Robbinsville, North Carolina in the southeastern United States. Wikipedia

This is the longest day ride that we include in our series. This ride is seven hours actual saddle time and can be up to nine hours with stops to eat and to gas up. The route is 283 miles of winding mountainous roads. The temperatures can vary greatly from the bottom of the skyway to the top, so be prepared!

The route on the map begins and ends in Talking Rock, GA. The beginning of the ride will send you north on Hwy 515/76 through Blue Ridge and on to Blairsville, GA. While in Blairsville, I suggest that you stop at Union PowerSports and say hello to George (the Owner) and all of the friendly staff there. NOTE: Be careful, they just might succeed in selling you a Honda Goldwing – not that I would know this first hand or anything! Upon leaving Blairsville, you will take Hwy 129 to NC Hwy 64/74 in Murphy, NC.. At this intersection turn right onto Hwy 64/74 and follow Hwy 74 through Andrews, NC, and then pick up Hwy 129 to Robbinsville, NC.. Just outside of Robbinsville, you will follow the signs leading you to the Cherohala Skyway. The Cherohala Skyway will bring you to Hwy 68 in Tellico Plains, TN. Turn right onto Hwy 68 and follow it out Madisonville, TN and Hwy 411. There are several good places to eat in Tellico Plains and Madisonville. From Madisonville, you will head south on Hwy 411 into Georgia all the way to Ranger, where you pick up Hwy 136 back to Talking Rock.

If you are looking for a place to spend the night and need a motel someplace during this ride, we recommend:

Best Western of Murphy
1522 Andrews Road
Murphy, NC 28906
828-837-3060

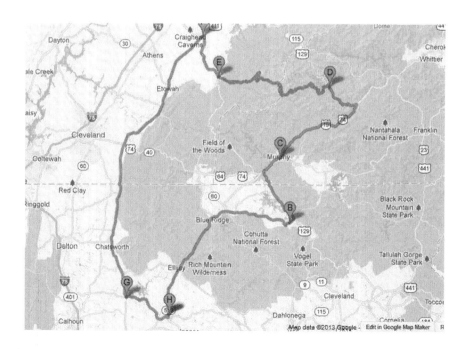

Below are turn by turn directions for this ride:

Bigun's Barbeque 362 Carnes Mill Rd Talking Rock, GA 30175

1.	Head northwest on Carnes Mill Rd toward State Route 515	0.1 mi
2.	Take the 1st right onto State Route 515	46.9 mi
3.	Turn right onto Kelly Rd	0.5 mi
4.	Continue onto Kelly Rd	285 ft
5.	Continue onto Kuituestia Creek Rd	0.7 mi
6.	Turn left onto Blue Ridge Hwy	1.2 mi
7.	Turn right onto Old Blue Ridge Hwy Destination will be on the right	177 ft

Union Powersports 1741 Blue Ridge Highway Blairsville, GA 30512

8.	Head northeast on Old Blue Ridge Hwy toward Blue Ridge Hwy	177 ft
9.	Turn right onto Blue Ridge Hwy	1.7 mi
10.	Turn right onto GA-2 E/US-76 E	0.1 mi
11.	Turn left onto GA-11 N/US-129 N/US-19 N Continue to follow US-129 N/US-19 N Entering North Carolina	14.3 mi

12. Turn right onto US-129 N/US-19 N/US-64 E/US-74 E   5.6 mi

U.S. 74 & U.S. 129 Murphy, NC 28906

13. Head east on US-129 N/US-19 N/US-74 E toward Ledford   24.1 mi

14. Turn left onto US-129 N/Tallulah Rd Continue to follow US-129 N   12.4 mi

U.S. 129 & N Carolina 143 Robbinsville, NC 28771

15. Head north on N Carolina 143 W/US-129 N/Tapoco Rd toward Sandhole Rd   0.5 mi

16. Turn left onto N Carolina 143 W/County Rd 1116/Cherohala Skyway   3.4 mi

17. Turn right onto N Carolina 143 W/County Rd 1127/Cherohala Skyway   6.8 mi

18. Turn left onto N Carolina 143 W/Cherohala Skyway Continue to follow Cherohala Skyway Entering Tennessee   41.6 mi

Tennessee 68 & Tennessee 165 Tellico Plains, TN 37385

19. Head north on TN-68 N toward Bears Ln 12.5 mi

Tennessee 68 & Old US Highway 411 Madisonville, TN 37354

20. Head southwest on Englewood Rd toward Station St   0.4 mi

21. Continue onto TN-33 S/US-411 S Continue to follow US-411 S Entering Georgia Destination will be on the left   73.5 mi

U.S. 411 GA

22.	Head south on GA-61 S/US-411 S toward GA-136 W/Nicklesville Rd NE	33 ft
23.	Take the 1st left onto GA-136 E/Hwy 136 W/Nicklesville Rd NE Continue to follow GA-136 E/Hwy 136 W	14.4 mi
24.	Turn left toward State Route 515	0.2 mi
25.	Turn left onto State Route 515	0.7 mi
26.	Take the 1st right onto Carnes Mill Rd Destination will be on the left	0.1 mi

Bigun's Barbeque 362 Carnes Mill Rd Talking Rock, GA 30175

On Saturday, September 19, 2009, 10 brave individuals decided that the strong rains of the week and day were not going to discourage them from making the long anticipated trip over the Cherohala Skyway. The rains had come and flooded Atlanta and much of North Georgia and yet some came from the metro area to ride!

The weather forecast was for showers and hard downpours for the entire day, but as we left Ellijay, the weather broke and we had semi-clear skies all of the way to the top of the Skyway, where we ran in to fog and clouds. Yes, clouds! At its peak, the Skyway is around 5400 ft. above sea level. It is truly a Skyway a mile in the Sky!

As we ventured down from the 40°+ temperature on the top of the mountains to the 75° temperatures in Tellico Plains, TN, we said our good-byes to 2 members of our group as they returned home by way of a different route, while the rest of us went into Madisonville, TN. and ate lunch and had a great time of fellowship around the table. When we emerged from the restaurant with our bellies full, we mounted up and headed south towards Georgia, only to have the rain finally catch us.

Even with the on and off again rain showers, everyone reported having a great ride!

Below are some pictures from the ride.

Getting ready to leave

Pulling out for the ride

Pulling out for the ride

Pulling out for the ride

Stops on the Cherohala Skyway

Stops on the Cherohala Skyway

Mountain views on the Skyway

Mountain views on the Skyway

4 LITTLE BAVARIA – HELEN, GA

Helen, GA is one of those mountain towns that we have watched over the past 30 years change from a sleepy little town with little craft shops, woodworkers, handmade dulcimer instrument makers, German restaurants and fudge making candy shops into more of a commercialized touristy souvenir shopping mecca. Don't get me wrong, Helen is a wonderfully fun place to visit. It has just changed.

One of the biggest changes that we have seen is the transformation into what I would call the Summer Biker Capital of Georgia! With the North Georgia Mountains being a favorite spot for bikers to travel to for the twisties, Helen has been discovered to sit right in the middle of them and seems to make sense as a popular stopping point where one can enjoy the mountains and the beginning cold waters of the Chattahoochee River.

The Chattahoochee River provides plenty of summer fun for all with its tubing, wading/swimming and trout fishing available in town and either side of town.

For the motorcyclists that find their way to Helen, they can always find themselves a good stopping point at the Chattahoochee Biker Gear location. Chattahoochee Biker Gear is located on the Cleveland side of town and really is about three shops in one. You can find just about any kind of apparel, patch, leather goods or helmets in this store that you may be looking for. When you are in Helen, be sure to stop by and see Pat or Carrie – you'll be glad you did!

Helen also offers a number of fun places to eat and hang out from Bavarian food to just a good old-fashion burger. During the summer months several of the restaurants offer biker nights with live music. This little town should not be overlooked on your journeys to the mountains!

From Helen, you can work your way to Unicoi State Park on your way to Lake Burton and Clayton. GA. Unicoi State Park has a lodge and restaurant that will cater to your every need and desire in the mountains. The last time that I was at the restaurant at the lodge, they had a buffet dinner that was absolutely delicious. At that time they prided themselves as being one of the only state park lodges to serve mountain fresh rainbow trout on their buffet!

From Unicoi, you can continue on and wind up going around Lake Burton and the outskirts of Clayton, GA. Lake Burton is home to the largest population of yellow perch in the state. Yellow perch in my opinion are the best eating fresh water game fish that you can catch.

After leaving the waters of Lake Burton behind, you will work your way back towards Hiawassee and another one of Georgia's great lakes. Lake Chatuge is another must see lake in beautiful mountain settings. As you follow along the lake heading south on Hwy 76, you will find the little towns of Young Harris, Blairsville, Blue Ridge, Ellijay and Jasper before entering the metro Atlanta area on Hwy I-575.

Getting to Helen can include some other wonderful little towns which we will cover in another chapter, but suffice it to say that in this chapter, we will reach Helen by way of the Richard B. Russell Parkway. This is one of the best riding roads in the state! You will have a blast here!

Enjoy as I list the routes to travel to get to "Little Bavaria".

July 18th 2009 Ride to Helen, GA

On Saturday morning, the sun rose early and chased the rain and clouds away from Friday evening. When I got up and went out to get the bike out of the barn for the morning's ride, the temperature was in the low 60's. What a beautiful day for a ride in the middle of July!

I knew that if it was this cool in Ellijay at 7:30 in the morning, we were going to have a perfect day to ride through the mountains to Helen and then on to Lake Burton and Clayton, GA. Boy, was I right! We could not have asked for a better day.

I figured that I would go on down to Scott's Corner Cafe at 8:30 and be the first one there to eat before the 10:00 AM ride. To my surprise, when I arrived, there was already a Goldwing sitting out front of the restaurant. Sure enough, somebody had already beaten me there for breakfast. Soon more riders began showing up and one by one they came and sat down to eat and get to know one another.

A few minutes after 10:00 AM, the kickstands went up and we were on our way. I had been right; as we started out the cool morning air was enough to make me wish that I had put my wind breaker on.

Needless to say, the ride to Helen was absolutely wonderful and the trip from Helen to Clayton past Lake Burton was awesome with the mountains towering out in front of us and the lake beside us. What a picture perfect ride!

Many years ago, my wife and I used to spend a lot of time in Helen and found it to be the nice little mountain town with lots of little craft shops and restaurants. Boy, have things changed! While there arc still little shops, restaurants and tubing on the river, Helen has become the Biker Capital of Georgia! There are several biker related shops there and all kinds of eating places catering to the bikers. The place that we ate at had a deck overlooking the river, with a roof overhead and stage area with a live band. They pride themselves as having the largest deck in Georgia!

Many thanks to all that came and made this trip so enjoyable! Please enjoy the pictures below!

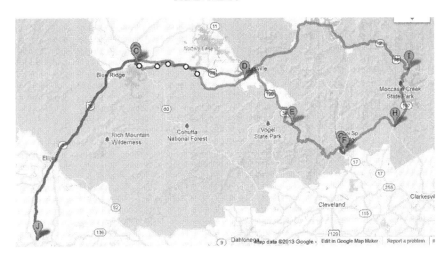

Below are turn by turn directions for this ride:

Bigun's Barbeque 362 Carnes Mill Rd Talking Rock, GA 30175

1. Head northwest on Carnes Mill Rd toward State Route 515   0.1 mi

2. Take the 1st right onto State Route 515   32.0 mi

3. Turn left onto GA-60 N/Lakewood Hwy Destination will be on the right   62 ft

Georgia 515 & Georgia 60 Mineral Bluff, GA 30559

4. Head southeast on GA-60 S/Lakewood Hwy toward GA-2/US-76/Appalachian Hwy Continue to follow GA-60 S   0.5 mi

5. Turn left onto GA-60 S/Old Hwy 76   285 ft

Georgia 60 & Old Highway 76 Mineral Bluff, GA 30559

6. Head east on GA-60 S/Old Hwy 76 toward Adra Dr Continue to follow Old Hwy 76 — 6.5 mi

7. Slight right toward Blue Ridge Hwy — 2.9 mi

8. Continue straight onto Blue Ridge Hwy — 9.2 mi

9. Turn right onto Old Blue Ridge Hwy Destination will be on the right — 177 ft

Union Powersports 1741 Blue Ridge Highway Blairsville, GA 30512

10. Head northeast on Old Blue Ridge Hwy toward Blue Ridge Hwy — 177 ft

11. Turn right onto Blue Ridge Hwy — 1.6 mi

12. Turn right onto Blue Ridge St — 0.6 mi

13. At the traffic circle, take the 2nd exit onto GA-11 S/US-129 S/US-19 S/Cleveland St Continue to follow GA-11 S/US-129 S/US-19 S — 7.5 mi

14. Turn left onto State Route 180 — 0.9 mi

15. Take the 2nd right onto GA-348 E/Richard B Russell Scenic Hwy — 3.2 mi

Richard B Russell Scenic Hwy Blairsville, GA 30512

16. Head east on GA-348 E/Richard B Russell Scenic Hwy toward Forest Srv Rd — 10.8 mi

17. Turn left onto GA-75Alt S — 2.3 mi

18. Turn right onto GA-17 S/GA-75 S/Unicoi Turnpike Destination will be on the left — 1.2 mi

Chattahoochee Biker Gear 8610 N Main St Helen, GA 30545

19. Head west on GA-17 N/GA-75 N/N Main St/Unicoi Turnpike toward Yonah St — 0.9 mi

Georgia 75 & Georgia 356 Helen, GA 30545

20. Head north on GA-356 E toward McFain Ln 10.8 mi

Georgia 197 & Georgia 356 Clarkesville, GA 30523

21. Head north on GA-197 N toward Goshen Creek Rd 11.5 mi

GA-197 N

22. Head north on GA-2 W/US-76 W/Lookout Mountain Scenic Hwy toward Popcorn Rd Continue to follow US-76 W — 70.4 mi

23. Continue onto GA-515 W/State Hwy 515 W/State Route 515 W/Hwy 515 W/Rte 515 W/State 515 W — 11.8 mi

24. Turn left onto Carnes Mill Rd Destination will be on the left — 0.1 mi

Bigun's Barbeque 362 Carnes Mill Rd Talking Rock, GA 30175

Helen, GA

Helen, GA

Helen, GA

A stop in Hiawassee, GA

This trip is roughly 191 miles in length from start to finish and takes approximately 4 hours and 10 minutes actual riding time under ideal conditions. This does not include any times for stopping at places to eat, shop or do tourist's things.

.

Chattahoochee Biker Gear sells everything motorcycle related except bikes (so far). We started with a small basement store in Helen, GA., 11 years ago. We quickly outgrew that location and moved to a store in Helen almost 4 times the size. With the demand for great biker gear competitively priced we ended up moving again in 2010 to our present location which represents 6,000 square feet of the largest selection of biker gear in the area. We also sell and sew patches on our apparel daily in our store.

Chattahoochee Biker Gear
8065 South Main St.
Helen, GA 30545
706-878-0076

Biker's Welcome!

Wildcat Lodge and Campground
7475 Georgia Hwy 60
Suches, GA 30572
(706) 747-1011

GPS Coordinates - +34° 43' 11.52", -84° 4' 1.54"

5 LAKE WEISS

This ride will take you across the northwestern part of the state from Talking Rock, GA through Rome, GA and on into AL.

Lake Weiss is a beautiful lake in northeast Alabama near Gadsden. The lake is very popular with anglers from all over the south, as it is home to trophy Crappie and is also a great Bass fishing lake. When you look at a map, the lake is almost on the Georgia border and it is a very large lake that during the summer months draws people for every type of sport imaginable.

This ride has become one of the favorites of our monthly riding group, as it gives you some great country riding, an opportunity to stop and shop or eat in a fairly decent-sized city as it passes through Rome, GA. Upon leaving Rome, the road just smoothes out for a nice back country ride until you reach Cedar Bluff, AL. Cedar Bluff reminds me of one of those quiet fishing towns that are magnificently situated on the shores of the lake! Upon leaving Cedar Bluff, you will cross a causeway over the lake and find yourself in Centre, AL which is located just twenty five miles from Gadsden, AL.

What I have found over the years, is that many people have heard of Lake Weiss (especially if you are a Crappie fisherman), but have never been there. Centre, AL sits on the shores of Lake Weiss and has a wonderful BBQ restaurant that will answer the call of any appetite! If you ever travel there during the weekdays, I would highly recommend Lanny's BBQ. In doing research and speaking with them, I have found that they have now closed on the weekends, so make sure to visit them on a weekday.

Centre is roughly 25 miles east of Gadsden, AL and could be added to the trip for an extended ride on your own.

The ride route is actually a very easy route to follow and you do go through the city of Rome by way of the bypass near Berry College, but the ride getting from Talking Rock to Rome and from Rome to Centre are some of the best non-mountainous roads that I have ridden in a while. Leaving Talking Rock and heading to Fairmont, GA, you do encounter some minor mountain roads for about 20 miles.

The ride starts at BigUn's BBQ located at 362 Carnes Mill Road, Talking Rock, GA 30175 (706) 253-7675 for a morning ride over to Centre. Arrive early if you would like to grab a biscuit or some breakfast.

The trip will take you across Hwy 136 to Hwy 53 into Fairmont and on into Rome. In Rome you pick up the bypass and take it to GA Hwy 20 W which becomes AL 9-S through Cedar Bluff, AL on the east shore of Lake Weiss and on into Centre on the west shore. For the return trip you will reverse your route. The route is 90 miles one way.

Below are the trip map picture and some photos from a May 2012 ride.

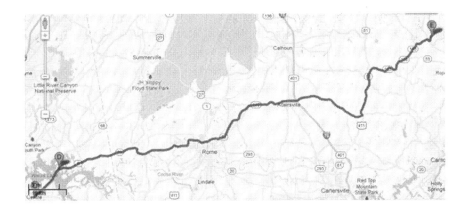

Lake Weiss

Lake Weiss

Lake Weiss

Lake Weiss

Below are turn by turn directions for this ride.

Bigun's Barbeque 362 Carnes Mill Rd Talking Rock, GA 30175

1. Head northwest on Carnes Mill Rd toward State Route 515 — 0.1 mi

2. Turn left onto GA-5 S/GA-515 W/State Hwy 5 S/State Hwy 515 W/State Route 5 S/State Route 515 W/Hwy 5 S/Hwy 515 W/Rte 5 S/Rte 515 W/State 5 S/State 515 W — 0.8 mi

3. Take the 1st right toward GA-136 W — 0.2 mi

4. Take the 1st right onto GA-136 W — 2.4 mi

5. Continue onto Georgia 136 Connector S — 2.6 mi

6. Slight right onto GA-53 W — 9.0 mi

7. Turn left onto GA-61 S/US-411 S/Salacoa Ave Continue to follow GA-61 S/US-411 S — 7.2 mi

8. Turn right onto GA-140 W/Henry Mack Hill Rd Continue to follow GA-140 W — 20.8 mi

9. Turn left onto GA-53 W/New Calhoun Hwy NE — 8.0 mi

10. Turn right onto State Loop 1 — 5.3 mi

11. Turn left onto Redmond Cir/State Loop 1 — 1.0 mi

12. Turn right onto GA-20 W/Shorter Ave NW Continue to follow GA-20 W Entering Alabama — 14.2 mi

13. Continue onto AL-9 S/State Route 9 S — 9.2 mi

14. Turn right onto S Weiss Lake Dr — 0.2 mi

15. Turn left onto Old Alabama 9 — 43 ft

Cedar Bluff, AL

16. Head east on Old Alabama 9 toward N Weiss Lake Dr — 43 ft

17. Take the 1st right onto S Weiss Lake Dr — 0.2 mi

18. Turn right onto AL-68 W/State Route 9 S Continue to follow AL-68 W — 5.5 mi

19. Continue onto AL-283 S/Cedar Bluff Rd Continue to follow AL-283 S — 0.7 mi

20. Make a U-turn at W Main St — 180 ft

Centre, AL

21. Head north on AL-283 N/Cedar Bluff Rd toward N River St Continue to follow AL-283 N — 0.7 mi

22. Continue onto Cedar Bluff Rd — 3.0

mi

23. Continue onto AL-68 E/AL-9 N/State Route 9 N	2.5 mi
24. Turn left onto S Weiss Lake Dr	0.2 mi
25. Turn left onto Old Alabama 9	43 ft

Cedar Bluff, AL

26. Head east on Old Alabama 9 toward N Weiss Lake Dr	43 ft
27. Take the 1st right onto S Weiss Lake Dr	0.2 mi
28. Turn left onto AL-9 N/State Route 9 N Entering Georgia	9.3 mi
29. Continue onto GA-20 E	14.1 mi
30. Turn left onto Redmond Cir/State Loop 1	1.0 mi
31. Slight right to stay on Redmond Cir/State Loop 1 Continue to follow State Loop 1	5.3 mi
32. Turn left onto GA-53 E/New Calhoun Hwy NE	8.0 mi
33. Turn right onto GA-140 E/Adairsville Rd NE Continue to follow GA-140 E	20.8 mi
34. Turn left onto GA-61 N/US-411 N	7.2 mi
35. Turn right onto GA-53 E/S R 35 Continue to follow GA-53 E	9.0 mi

36. Turn left onto Georgia 136 Connector N · · · · · · · · · · · 2.6 mi

37. Continue onto GA-136 E · 2.4 mi

38. Turn left toward State Route 515 · · · · · · · · · · · · · · · 0.2 mi

39. Turn left onto State Route 515 · · · · · · · · · · · · · · · · · 0.7 mi

40. Take the 1st right onto Carnes Mill Rd Destination will be on the left · 0.1 mi

Bigun's Barbeque 362 Carnes Mill Rd Talking Rock, GA 30175

The distance of this ride is approximately 90 miles each way and takes roughly two hours actual riding time each way.

Take your time and enjoy a beautiful day at the lake!

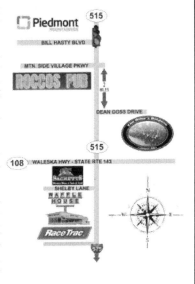

Dairy Queen
1043 S Main St,
Ellijay, GA 30540
(706) 635-2020

6 EUHARLEE'S COVERED BRIDGE

As I write this chapter, I have included a brief description below that was published in the "Born to Ride" magazine in February 2013. I make mention of a couple of businesses that are worth your stopping at, as well as a small description of the bridge museum. Let me just say here, that if you have never been to the museum, it is well worth the ride. On the way, you will go through Cartersville, GA which in itself is quite a nice place to visit and you can easily spend several hours there.

Cartersville is home to a very nice Harley Davidson shop that is a nice breaking point on this ride. Even though I ride a Goldwing and my wife rides a Kawasaki (you Harley riders will just have to forgive us), we still enjoy stopping at Cartersville Harley Davidson and looking around and my wife seems to like spending money there in spite of the fact that we do not own a Harley! I have a feeling, if she has her way, her next bike just might be a Harley.

In addition to the Harley Shop, Cartersville is home to the Booth Western Art Museum that is well worth the visit. We recently rode over and went through the museum and if you are at all interested in the history of the Wild West, Indian History or Civil War history, this place must be on your bucket list!

One last thing that I will mention about Cartersville is that they have done a wonderful job of restoring the main downtown section from the old theater and little shops either side of it to the railroad depot. Cartersville was and still is a major railroad town for any of you who may have an interest in trains. In its early days, Cartersville was where different railroads came together and interchanged with each other. Today, the differing lines still exist, but are all under the control of CSX Corporation. There are about four rail yards in Cartersville that are of notable size (three of which technically make up one yard – two on the old individual lines and one where the two lines join together). There are several smaller yards and sidings along the industrial sections of town. There is still plenty of rail traffic coming through Cartersville every day. Cartersville is truly a rail fan's paradise.

The ride from Cartersville out to Euharlee is just a short ride of about fifteen minutes, but will take you through some nice rural faming land. It is just a nice pleasant ride, but off in the distance, you will see huge towers encroaching on the skyline of little Euharlee. At first glance, you think that these are nuclear cooling towers and in fact they are cooling towers, but not nuclear. Euharlee is also home to Plant Bowen. Plant Bowen has the second largest generating capacity of any coal-fired power plant in North America, and the largest in the United States. Plant Bowen is owned by Georgia Power. Bowen's four cooling towers are 381 ft (116 m) tall and 318 ft (97 m) in diameter and can cool 1,100,000 US gallons (4,200,000 l; 920,000 imp gal) per minute. Another 26,000 US gallons (98,000 l; 22,000 imp gal) of water is lost to evaporation which creates the distinctive white clouds rising from each tower. (Source Wikipedia) Plant Bowen also has two smokestacks that are 1,001' high each. This is a sight that you will not miss!

Plant Bowen

Just down the road about two miles from Plant Bowen is the Euharlee Covered Bridge Museum. The Euharlee Covered Bridge, also known as the Euharlee Creek Covered Bridge or rarely the Lowry Bridge, is a wooden Town Lattice covered bridge crossing Euharlee Creek in Euharlee. The bridge was built in 1886 by Horace King's son Washington King and Johnathan H. Burke. The bridge spans 138 feet. The lattice trusses consist of planks crisscrossing at 45- to 60-degree angles and are fastened with wooden pegs, or trunnels, at each intersection. Traffic finally stopped across the bridge in 1980 when a new two-lane bridge was built. (Source Wikipedia)

Euharlee's Covered Bridge

Upon leaving the Covered Bridge Museum, we will continue on to Rome, GA, where I recommend stopping and eating at Fuddruckers Restaurant. This is located on the bypass loop close to the Martha Berry Parkway. Berry College is located just a short distance north of the intersection of Loop 1 (bypass) and Martha Berry Parkway (Hwy 27) and is a beautiful college campus.

Berry College is a private, four-year liberal arts college located in Mount Berry, Floyd County, Georgia, just north of Rome. It is accredited by the Southern Association of Colleges and Schools (SACS). Berry was founded in 1902 by Martha Berry, and, boasting 27,000 acres (110 km²), Berry is now the largest contiguous campus in the world. The Berry campus consists of fields, forests, and Lavender Mountain. Designated portions are open to the public for hiking, cycling, horseback riding, and other outdoor activities. The campus is also home to a large population of deer (estimates range between 1,500 and 2,500). The Georgia Department of Natural Resources oversees about 16,000 acres of the campus, conducts managed hunts and provides recreational opportunities within the department of regulations. However, land encompassing the academic buildings and other public spaces is a wildlife refuge in which no hunting is allowed.

Berry was founded in 1902 by Martha McChesney Berry as a school for rural boys. Seven years later, a girl's school was added. A junior college was established in 1926, and a four-year college followed in 1930. Graduate programs outside the liberal arts were added in 1972. Funds for campus facilities and other programs have been provided by such notable contributors as Henry Ford and Truett Cathy. (Source Wikipedia)

Berry College

Our ride will begin at BigUn's BBQ in Talking Rock where we will pick up Hwy 136 to Hwy 53 and on into Fairmont. In Fairmont, we will ride Hwy 411 to Cartersville and make a short stop at Harley Davidson of Cartersville.

After leaving the Harley shop in Cartersville, we will continue into town and pick up Hwy 113 to Euharlee Rd. out to the Museum. If you have never been to Euharlee, you will discover that the museum is home to the oldest covered bridge in the state, and it has not been moved from its original location. The museum has a nice little park area, just perfect for a break from the ride! Upon completing our short break in Euharlee, we will work our way out to Hwy 411 and head for Rome, where I recommended a stop for some lunch at Fuddruckers, across from the Braves Stadium on the Rome Bypass near Berry College.

The final leg of the trip will take us from Rome on Hwy 53 to Calhoun, GA where we will pick up Redbud Road (this is Hwy 156 and it goes beneath I-75, so anyone desiring to break off can do so). The remainder will ride back to Hwy 411 to Hwy 136 and Hwy 382 back to Ellijay.

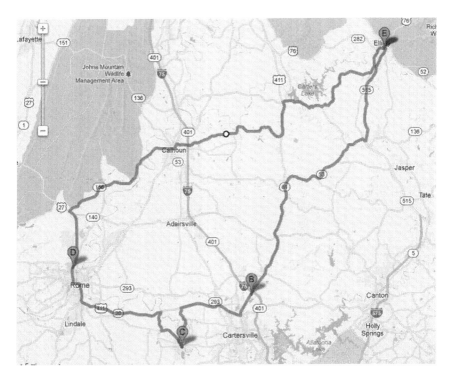

Here are turn by turn directions for this ride:

Bigun's Barbeque 362 Carnes Mill Rd Talking Rock, GA 30175

1. Head northwest on Carnes Mill Rd toward State Route 515   0.1 mi

2. Turn left onto GA-5 S/GA-515 W/State Hwy 5 S/State Hwy 515 W/State Route 5 S/State Route 515 W/Hwy 5 S/Hwy 515 W/Rte 5 S/Rte 515 W/State 5 S/State 515 W | 0.8 mi

3. Take the 1st right toward GA-136 W | 0.2 mi

4. Take the 1st right onto GA-136 W | 2.4 mi

5. Continue onto Georgia 136 Connector S | 2.6 mi

6. Slight right onto GA-53 W | 9.0 mi

7. Turn left onto GA-61 S/US-411 S/Salacoa Ave Continue to follow GA-61 S/US-411 S | 15.4 mi

8. Turn right onto Old Henderson Rd NE Destination will be on the left | 0.1 mi

Harley-Davidson-Cartersville 2281 U.S. 411 Cartersville, GA 30121

9. Head east on Old Henderson Rd NE toward GA-61 S/US-411 S | 0.1 mi

10. Turn right onto GA-61 S/US-411 S | 3.0 mi

11. Slight right to merge onto GA-20 W/GA-3 N/U.S. 41 N/US-411 S/Joe Frank Harris Pkwy SE toward Kingston/Rome | 3.0 mi

12. Take the ramp onto GA-20 W/US-411 S | 5.4

mi

13.	Turn left onto Harden Bridge Rd SW/Hardin Bridge Rd Continue to follow Hardin Bridge Rd	4.7 mi
14.	Turn left onto Euharlee Rd SW	0.6 mi
15.	Take the 2nd right onto Covered Bridge Rd SW/Euharlee Rd Destination will be on the right	0.4 mi

Euharlee Covered Bridge 116 Covered Bridge Rd SW Euharlee, GA 30120

16.	Head northwest on Covered Bridge Rd SW/Euharlee Rd toward Euharlee 5 Forks Rd SW	0.4 mi
17.	Turn left onto Euharlee Rd SW	3.4 mi
18.	Turn right onto Macedonia Rd	2.6 mi
19.	Turn left onto GA-20 W/US-411 S	10.7 mi
20.	Take the US 27/Georgia 53/Georgia 20 ramp to Rome	0.2 mi
21.	Merge onto US-27 N/E 2nd Ave Continue to follow US-27 N	2.1 mi
22.	Turn left onto Broad St	0.2 mi
23.	Take the 2nd right onto Riverside Pkwy NE	1.8 mi
24.	Make a U-turn at State Loop 1/Veterans Memorial Pkwy NE Destination will be on the right	400 ft

Fuddruckers 595 Riverside Pkwy NE Rome, GA 30161

25.	Head south on Riverside Pkwy NE toward Chatillon Rd	13 ft
26.	Take the 1st left onto Chatillon Rd	0.2 mi
27.	Turn left onto J L Todd Dr	0.2 mi
28.	Turn right onto State Loop 1/Veterans Memorial Pkwy NE Continue to follow State Loop 1	1.6 mi
29.	Turn left onto GA-53 E	18.2 mi
30.	Turn left onto S River St	1.5 mi
31.	Turn right onto Court St	0.2 mi
32.	Turn left onto N Wall St	0.6 mi
33.	Turn right toward College St	463 ft
34.	Turn left onto College St	338 ft
35.	Slight right onto Old Red Bud Rd	0.1 mi

Old Red Bud Rd Calhoun, GA 30701

36.	Head southwest on Old Red Bud Rd toward Nelson St	131 ft
37.	Take the 1st right onto Nelson St	0.1 mi
38.	Turn right onto GA-3 N/U.S. 41 N/N Wall St Continue to follow GA-3 N/U.S. 41 N	1.3 mi

39. Slight right toward GA-225 N	203 ft
40. Continue straight onto GA-225 N	7.3 mi
41. Turn right onto GA-136 E/Nicklesville Rd NE Continue to follow GA-136 E	15.6 mi
42. Turn left onto GA-382 E	4.7 mi

Georgia 382 Ellijay, GA 30540

43. Head northeast on GA-382 E toward Barnes Mountain Rd	5.3 mi
44. Turn right to stay on GA-382 E	1.5 mi
45. Turn left to stay on GA-382 E	420 ft
46. Take the 1st right onto GA-5 S/GA-515 W/State Hwy 5 S/State Hwy 515 W/State Route 5 S/State Route 515 W/Hwy 5 S/Hwy 515 W/Rte 5 S/Rte 515 W/State 5 S/State 515 W	6.6 mi
47. Turn left onto Carnes Mill Rd Destination will be on the left	0.1 mi

Bigun's Barbeque 362 Carnes Mill Rd Talking Rock, GA 30175

Cartersville Harley-Davidson

Euharlee Covered Bridge Museum

Euharlee Covered Bridge Museum

Euharlee Covered Bridge Museum

Euharlee Covered Bridge Museum

Cartersville Harley-Davidson

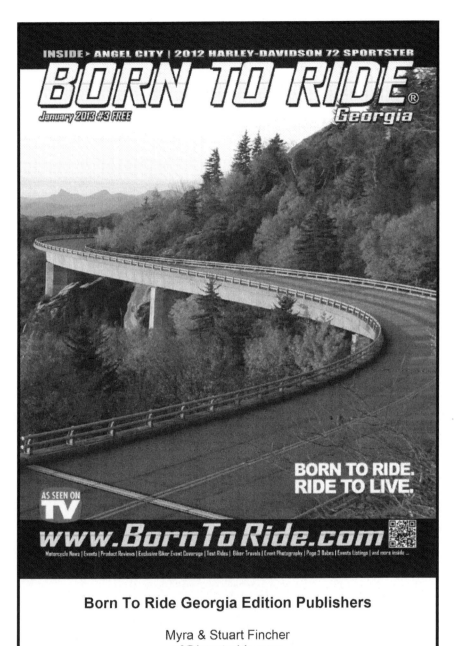

Born To Ride Georgia Edition Publishers

Myra & Stuart Fincher
sf@borntoride.com
Office: 706-865-4140

7 CHICKAMAUGA BATTLE FIELD

What a beautiful day today was! I started the day planning to sit down and write this article, but the weather outside kept looking nicer and nicer and the temps just kept rising. I knew that I needed to get this article written, but a day like this in February just needs to be ridden. I purposed that I would not let it get the best of me and that I would write – then it happened; my son came out of his room and announced that he and a friend were going to ride their bikes to Cumming by way of Dawsonville! That's all it took – I was outa here. I decided that I would ride as far as Dawsonville and call on one of my customers there that I have needed to see. Six hours, 67° and 100+ miles later, I am finally sitting down and writing!

Stuart Fincher, publisher of "Born to Ride" magazine, and I talked about doing some articles and rides that would take us to some historical places around the state. Our ride that appeared in the February issue and was ridden in March, 2013 took us to the Euharlee Covered Bridge Museum, just outside of Cartersville, GA. I have been doing a lot of thinking about this and have looked at several rides in different parts of the state, like the Uncle Remus Museum in Eatonton, GA and the Georgia Agarama in Tifton, GA as some examples. Of course, my wife and I just came back from a cruise on Thursday (today is Saturday) that took us to Key West and the Bahamas. Key West is a very historical town, but unfortunately is not in GA. However if you watch my www.northgeorgiamotorcycles.com website, you might just find a week-long tour appearing in the near future!

Our ride will give you two historical bangs for your buck! We will be traveling to the Chickamauga Battlefield in Ringgold, GA. We also we be taking you to meet a historical figure in the motorcycling community, Tammy Jo Kirk. Tammy is the owner of Kirk's Cycles in Dalton, GA and she was not only a first for women in motorcycle racing, but also NASCAR and the Craftsman Truck Series of auto racing.

Tammy Jo Kirk (born May 6, 1962 in Dalton, Georgia) is a racecar and motorcycle racer. She was the first woman to race in the NASCAR Craftsman Truck Series and later returned to NASCAR to run the Busch Series. She has not driven in NASCAR since 2003.

Kirk began her racing career in motorcycles at the age of 9, moving up through the ranks of the sport during her teenage years and finally reaching the peak of the sport, the A.M.A. Grand National Championship. She became the first woman in history to reach a Grand National Championship final when she earned a spot in the 1983 Knoxville Half Mile event. In 1986, she made history by winning a Class C flat track race in Knoxville, Tennessee.

After Kirk retired from motorcycle racing due to frustration about the refusal of companies to provide spare parts to a female competitor, she moved on to late model racing in 1989. Kirk joined the NASCAR Winston All-American Challenge Series in 1991, becoming the first female driver to compete in the series. In 1994, she was named the Most Popular Driver in the series, which had been renamed the Slim Jim All Pro Series, and she finished seventh in series points two years later. Kirk became the second woman to win a NASCAR touring series event (the first being Shawna Robinson in 1988) in the Goody's Dash Series when she won the 1994 Snowball Derby, which was at the time a points race in the All Pro Series. [Source: Wikipedia]

Tammy will welcome you at Kirk's Cycles in Dalton and will be available to meet everyone during your stop there, providing she is not out on a delivery or making an appearance somewhere.

Our ride will begin at BigUn's BBQ at the corner of Hwy 515 and Carnes Mill Road in Talking Rock, GA with Kick Stands Up at 10:00 AM. Our ride will travel across Hwy 136 to Hwy 411 to Chatsworth where we will follow Hwy 76 into Dalton and visit Kirk's Cycle. From Dalton, we will travel to Hwy 201 in Rocky Face and follow that to Hwy 136 and then proceed into Lafayette. In Lafayette, we will pick up Hwy 27 to the Battlefield. Upon Leaving the Battlefield, we will continue on Battlefield Parkway to Interstate 75 South. Those wishing to remain on I-75 to Atlanta may do so while the rest of the ride will exit onto Hwy 136 at Resaca and back to Talking Rock.

Tammy Jo Kirk

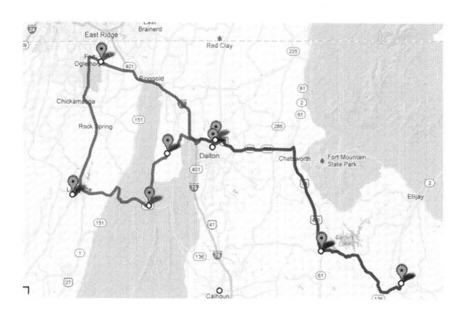

Below are turn by turn directions for this ride:

Bigun's Barbeque 362 Carnes Mill Rd Talking Rock, GA 30175

1.	Head northwest on Carnes Mill Rd toward State Route 515	0.1 mi
2.	Turn left onto GA-5 S/GA-515 W/State Hwy 5 S/State Hwy 515 W/State Route 5 S/State Route 515 W/Hwy 5 S/Hwy 515 W/Rte 5 S/Rte 515 W/State 5 S/State 515 W	0.8 mi
3.	Take the 1st right toward GA-136 W/Hwy 136 W	0.2 mi
4.	Take the 1st right onto GA-136 W/Hwy 136 W	14.4 mi
5.	Turn right onto GA-61 N/US-411 N Destination will be on the right	33 ft

U.S. 411 GA

6.	Head north on GA-61 N/US-411 N	14.5 mi
7.	Turn left onto GA-52 W/US-76 W/G I Maddox Pkwy Continue to follow GA-52 W/US-76 W	8.3 mi
8.	Turn right onto State Route 52C/US-76 W/Admiral Mack Gaston Pkwy/N Dalton Bypass Continue to follow US-76 W	3.5 mi
9.	Turn left onto N Glenwood Ave Destination will be on the right	0.9 mi

Kirk's Cycle LLC 929 N Glenwood Ave Dalton, GA 30721

10.	Head north on N Glenwood Ave toward E Park St	0.9 mi
11.	Turn left onto GA-3 N/U.S. 41 N/US-76 W/N Bypass	2.0 mi
12.	Turn right onto Willowdale Rd	0.8 mi
13.	Turn right onto GA-2/GA-3 N/U.S. 41 N/US-76 W/Chattanooga Rd	1.9 mi
14.	Turn left onto Ronald Ln	0.1 mi
15.	Continue onto GA-201 S/Lafayette Rd	3.2 mi

Georgia 201 Rocky Face, GA 30740

16.	Head south on GA-201 S/Lafayette Rd toward Dunnagan Rd Continue to follow GA-201 S	8.0 mi

Georgia 136 & Georgia 201 LaFayette, GA 30728

17.	Head southwest on GA-201 S toward GA-136 W	102 ft
18.	Take the 1st right onto GA-136 W	6.6 mi
19.	Turn left onto GA-136 W/GA-151 S/S Old Alabama Hwy	1.4 mi
20.	Turn right onto GA-136 W/E Villanow St Continue to follow E Villanow St	4.5 mi

21. Turn left onto S Main St · 0.3 mi

22. Turn right onto W Main St · 0.3 mi

23. Take the 2nd left onto S Chattanooga St · 0.8 mi

24. Turn right onto Spencer St Destination will be on the left · 0.2 mi

Hwy 27 GA

25. Head southeast on Spencer St toward Magnolia St · 0.2 mi

26. Turn left onto S Chattanooga St · 0.8 mi

27. Turn right onto W Main St · 0.3 mi

28. Turn left onto S Main St · 3.1 mi

29. Continue onto GA-1 N/US-27 N · 10.9 mi

30. Turn right onto Lafayette Rd · 4.7 mi

31. Turn right onto Battlefield Pkwy · 1.9 mi

Battlefield Pkwy Chickamauga, GA 30707

32. Head southeast on GA-2 E/Battlefield Pkwy · 4.4 mi

33. Take the ramp onto I-75 S · 14.3 mi

34.	Take exit 336 for US-41/US-76 toward Dalton/Rocky Face	0.1 mi
35.	Keep right at the fork, follow signs for US-41 S	184 ft
36.	Turn right onto U.S. 41 S/US-76 E/Chattanooga Rd Continue to follow US-76 E	3.0 mi

U.S. 76 Dalton, GA

37.	Head east on State Route 52C/US-76/Admiral Mack Gaston Pkwy/N Bypass toward Vista Dr Continue to follow State Route 52C/US-76/Admiral Mack Gaston Pkwy	3.1 mi
38.	Turn left onto GA-52 E/US-76 E/Chatsworth Rd SE Continue to follow GA-52 E/US-76 E	8.3 mi
39.	Turn right onto GA-61 S/US-411 S/N 3rd Ave Continue to follow GA-61 S/US-411 S Destination will be on the left	14.5 mi

U.S. 411 GA

40.	Head south on GA-61 S/US-411 S toward GA-136 W/Nicklesville Rd NE	33 ft
41.	Take the 1st left onto GA-136 E/Hwy 136 W/Nicklesville Rd NE Continue to follow GA-136 E/Hwy 136 W	14.4 mi
42.	Turn left toward State Route 515	0.2 mi
43.	Turn left onto State Route 515	0.7 mi
44.	Take the 1st right onto Carnes Mill Rd Destination will be on the left	0.1 mi

Bigun's Barbeque 362 Carnes Mill Rd Talking Rock, GA 30175

Firing of the canon about makes you come 2 feet off the ground!

Chickamauga Battlefield

Chickamauga Battlefield

Chickamauga Battlefield

On the way to the Chickamauga Battlefield

On the way to the Chickamauga Battlefield

8 TOCCOA FALLS

The ride that I am writing about here was actually our ride for the month of May, 2013 and will be part of a special weekend in Blue Ridge, GA as the WK Café & Grill (Waffle King), North Georgia Motorcycles and "Born to Ride" Magazine team up to bring you a two day fun filled rally. This rally is scheduled to become an annual event and should be held in May every year. This is a first for the city of Blue Ridge and several of the area merchants are going to be involved by helping to sponsor this event. There will tubing on the Toccoa River and Zip Line and Canopy Tours, as well as other activities over the weekend. The event will actually take place at the WK Café & Grill located on Hwy 515 in Blue Ridge.

On Saturday, at the Café, they will be having several vendors along with a bike judging competition. There are other activities including bike games and other events planned, as well as, our ride.

We will be leaving from WK Café & Grill for the ride to Helen and Toccoa. Plan to arrive early to get registered for events of the day and to grab some breakfast or lunch (brunch)!

Our ride will leave Blue Ridge and work our way to Blairsville by way of Old Hwy 2/76 where we will pick up the beautiful Richard B Russell Parkway across the mountains in to Helen, GA. While in Helen, we will stop at the Chattahoochee Biker Gear for a few minutes. From Helen, we will continue on to Toccoa, GA by way of Hwy 75 and Hwy 17. On the return from Toccoa we will travel Hwy 123 to Hwy 441, Hwy 105 to Hwy 115 and then to Hwy 129/19 and finally back to Hwy 76.

In Toccoa, we will give you the chance to visit Toccoa Falls on the campus of Toccoa Falls College. Toccoa Falls College was the site of the earthen dam brake in 1977 which claimed the lives of 39 students and faculty, when the water cascaded from the lake above the falls and created an instantaneous wall of water over the campus in the very early morning hours.

After our visit in Toccoa, we will return back to Blue Ridge by way of Cornelia and Cleveland. When we arrive back in Blue Ridge, Eddie and the staff at WK Café & Grill will be serving up everything from Sports Bar food items to steak inside or out on their deck. You will be able to enjoy a cold beer with your meal and settle in for an evening of entertainment, as you listen to the live bands on stage! If you find that the day has been too long or that maybe that cold brew just taste too good and you would like to stay the night, the Days Inn right next door will have rooms available for Saturday night.

On Sunday morning there will be a special biker church service and the blessing of the bikes, after which you can ride the mountains all over again. This time all on your own!

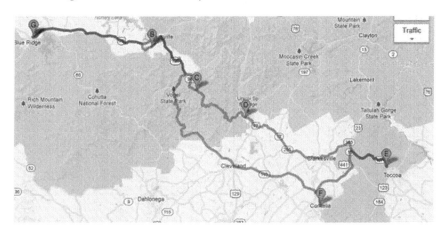

Below are turn by turn directions for this ride:

Royal Waffle King 4960 Georgia 515 Blue Ridge, GA 30513

1.	Head east on GA-2 E/US-76 E/Appalachian Hwy toward Orvin Lance Connector Continue to follow GA-2 E/US-76 E	18.0 mi
2.	Turn right onto Kelly Rd	0.5 mi
3.	Continue onto Kelly Rd	285 ft
4.	Continue onto Kuituestia Creek Rd	0.7 mi
5.	Turn left onto Blue Ridge Hwy	1.2 mi
6.	Turn right onto Old Blue Ridge Hwy Destination will be on the right	177 ft

Union Powersports 1741 Blue Ridge Highway Blairsville, GA 30512

7.	Head northeast on Old Blue Ridge Hwy toward Blue Ridge Hwy	177 ft
8.	Turn right onto Blue Ridge Hwy	1.6 mi
9.	Turn right onto Blue Ridge St	0.6 mi
10.	At the traffic circle, take the 2nd exit onto GA-11 S/US-129 S/US-19 S/Cleveland St Continue to follow GA-11 S/US-129 S/US-19 S	7.5 mi
11.	Turn left onto State Route 180	0.9 mi

| 12. | Take the 2nd right onto GA-348 E/Richard B Russell Scenic Hwy | 3.2 mi |

Richard B Russell Scenic Hwy Blairsville, GA 30512

13.	Head east on GA-348 E/Richard B Russell Scenic Hwy toward Forest Srv Rd	10.8 mi
14.	Turn left onto GA-75Alt S	2.3 mi
15.	Turn right onto GA-17 S/GA-75 S/Unicoi Turnpike Destination will be on the left	1.2 mi

Chattahoochee Biker Gear 8610 N Main St Helen, GA 30545

16.	Head east on GA-17 S/GA-75 S/N Main St/Unicoi Turnpike toward Spring Strasse Continue to follow GA-17 S/GA-75 S	2.0 mi
17.	Turn left onto GA-17 S/Unicoi Turnpike Continue to follow GA-17 S	11.2 mi
18.	Turn left onto GA-115 N/GA-17 S	1.9 mi
19.	Turn left onto U.S. 441 Historical N/Washington St	223 ft
20.	Take the 1st right onto GA-385 N/Grant St/U.S. 441 Historical N Continue to follow GA-385 N/U.S. 441 Historical N	5.3 mi
21.	Turn right onto GA-385 N/Talmadge Dr Continue to follow Talmadge Dr	3.6 mi
22.	Continue onto GA 17Alt S	4.9 mi

23. Turn right onto Forrest Dr	0.2	mi

Toccoa Falls College Stephens GA

24. Head east on Forrest Dr toward Old Clarksville Rd	0.2	mi
25. Turn left onto GA 17Alt N/Toccoa Falls Rd Sr17 Continue to follow GA 17Alt N	7.2	mi
26. Turn left onto Hollywood Hills Rd	0.3	mi
27. Take the 1st left onto GA-15 S/US-23 S/US-441 S	9.7	mi
28. Take exit 27 for U. S. 441 Historical/Georgia 105/Georgia 385 N toward Cornelia/Demorest	0.2	mi
29. Keep right at the fork, follow signs for US-441 BUS and merge onto GA-105 S/GA-15 S/US-441 BUS S/U.S. 441 Historical S	1.7	mi
30. Turn left onto Clarkesville St	0.5	mi
31. Turn right	52	ft

Cornelia, GA

32. Head west toward Main St NW	7 ft	
33. Turn right onto Main St NW	0.5	mi

34.	Turn right onto GA-105 N/US-441 BUS N/U.S. 441 Historical N/Veterans Memorial Dr Continue to follow GA-105 N/US-441 BUS N/U.S. 441 Historical N	2.2 mi
35.	Slight left onto GA-105 N/Cannon Bridge Rd Continue to follow GA-105 N	4.9 mi
36.	Turn left onto GA-115 S	9.0 mi
37.	Turn right onto GA-11 N/US-129 N/Courthouse Square Continue to follow GA-11 N/US-129 N	31.2 mi
38.	At the traffic circle, take the 4th exit onto Blue Ridge St	0.5 mi
39.	Turn right onto GA-11 N/US-129 N/US-19 N	0.1 mi
40.	Turn left onto GA-2 W/US-76 W	21.0 mi
41.	Make a U-turn at Windy Ridge Circle Destination will be on the right	492 ft

Royal Waffle King 4960 Georgia 515 Blue Ridge, GA 30513

I have decided to include a reprint about the dam break at Toccoa Falls here for you to read. This was a terrible event not only for the college, city and state, but also for our nation! I remember the day that this happened as it made the national news. I remember it so very well because, I was a freshman in college that year in Upstate New York and I remember thinking how it could have been me there at Toccoa Falls College!

What Happened the Night the Dam Broke

Toccoa, Ga. — The earthen dam above beautiful Toccoa Falls had been taken for granted for most of its 40 years. Through other winter and spring rains that come annually to the North Georgia Mountains, the tree covered dam had held.

About 1:30 a.m. Sunday, after days of torrential rains, the dam started to leak. Groaning under the pressure of 129 million gallons of water, the leak became a breach, and the dam washed away, sending a 30-foot wall of water roaring through the trailer park and Bible College in the peaceful valley below.

In a few horrifying minutes, at least 39 men, women, and children died in the onslaught of rushing water, wreckage and mud.

Sometime after midnight, Eldon Elsberry, Ron Ginther, Bill Ehrensberger, and David Fledderjohann,
started knocking on the doors of trailers to warn residents of the rising waters. Only Elsberry and Ginther would survive the night.

With a crashing sound like a thunderstorm, a wedge-shaped wall of water some 30 feet high poured down the creek and shot over Toccoa Falls, tumbling huge boulders and tree trunks before it.

The footbridge at the base of the falls vanished, as did the road that leads down the shoulder of the campus and across the creek to some recreational buildings. Just past the road, the creek makes a sharp left turn. On the outside of the bend sits Forrest Hall, with the windows of its basement rooms facing the stream. It was in that basement that three young men died. . . . Sweeping past Forrest Hall, the water churned through several houses, moved slightly to the right, or south, and washed headlong into [an area once know*n as*] *Trailerville.*

[A short distance away] it was the highway bridge, straddling the creek just below the city's hospital that contained the flood and kept it from wreaking havoc the length of the creek, Corps of Engineers workers said. Debris piled up against the bridge created a small dam, slowing the onrushing tide. (39 Die in Toccoa's Raging Nightmare." *The Atlanta Journal*, November 7, 1977.)

(Adapted from the booklet *In Darkness and Dawn* published by Toccoa Falls College Press)

All pictures of the damage caused by the flood are from the U.S. Geological Survey Photographic Library and are public domain.

Picture showing the breach in the earthen dam above the falls

Toccoa Falls following the dam break

Some of the aftermath of the dam break

Some of the remains of Trailerville beneath Toccoa Falls

This building is where the entrance to the falls is located

Toccoa Falls today!

Eric Wieberg

Your Trailer Connection in the North Georgia Mountains

"Our only BUSINESS is trailers and We stay behind you the whole Way!"

Cowboy Custom Trailers
1741 Blue Ridge Highway
Blairsville, Georgia 30512
706-835-2243

El Rey Cantina

945 Maddox Dr
Ellijay, GA 30540
706-276-1515

Business Info
Hours
Mon: 11:00 AM – 10:00 PM
Tue: 11:00 AM – 10:00 PM
Wed: 11:00 AM – 10:00 PM
Thu: 11:00 AM – 10:00 PM
Fri: 11:00 AM – 11:00 PM
Sat: 11:00 AM – 11:00 PM
Sun: 12:00 PM – 10:00 PM
Payments Accepted
American Express, Discover, MasterCard, Visa
Now Serving Alcoholic Beverages 7 Days a Week!

9 SUPPORT

In thinking about the title for this last chapter, I chose the title "SUPPORT" for several reasons. It comes at the end of this book and, as with just about with any item that you purchase, one of the last things that you will find in the back of the owner's manual, is a section entitled "SUPPORT".

I own a computer retail and repair shop in Ellijay, GA and I am very familiar with the term "SUPPORT"! In layman's terms, it simply means that you need my help or that I need your help. In other words, you need me and I need you!

How important this has become in America today! Given the state of our nation, both politically and economically, we need to stand together as one voice supporting each other! Now, I am not a real big fan of politics and let's just say that I really don't care what political party that you belong to, I just know that we have the opportunity to live in the greatest place on earth -"America"!

I have come to realize over the past few years, more than ever, bikers will come together and work together for a good cause more so than any other group that I know! We will come together in a poker run or charity ride for some group or individual that we don't even know – why – because, so many of us have been on the other side or we just know that we need each other in times of need. We come together to help fight against things that are unfair and unjust and we will come together to support those that have fought for our freedom and rights to agree or disagree!

THANK YOU TO ALL OF MY BROTHERS & SISTERS THAT HAVE SERVED THIS COUNTRY AND ARE PROUD TO BE CALLED AN AMERICAN VETERAN!

In this chapter, I also want to thank the local businesses in the communities in which we ride that are willing to stand up and say "we understand the values that the biking community holds to" and we welcome you into our business establishment.

In the past year, as I prepared for this book, it has been so amazing to find business men and women, who have told me that the biking community represents some of their best and best-mannered customers that they have! One example of this is the Best Western Motel in Murphy, NC, where Aurelia Stone, General Manager says that she welcomes all bikers. She goes so far as to welcome the bikers, that she makes certain to keep ride guides for the area available on the front counter, and when you spend the night, she gives you courtesy rags for your bike and also provides a wash station just for bikes. I also would like to add that Aurelia Stone is not a biker herself. She just enjoys having them come to her motel and visit with her!

This is a common theme among so many business owners and we just want to offer our "SUPPORT" to them. They need our business and we need or want the services that they offer. It's a Win-Win Situation.

Below is a listing of all businesses that are represented in this book and there are several more to be found on the website at http://www.northgeorgiamotorcycles.com. I have broken them down by category in order to make it easier to find what you are looking for!

Motorcycle Dealers and Shops:

Union Powersports, Inc.
1543 Old Blue Ridge Highway Blairsville GA 30512
Phone: 706.745.9671   Fax: 706.781.1906

Kirk's Cycle
929 N. Glenwood Ave.
Dalton, GA 30721
706-226-4090

Motorcycle Dealers and Shops:

Cycle Nation of Canton
645 Riverstone Parkway
Canton, GA 30114
770-720-9554

Riders Hill
3003 Morrison Moore Parkway E.
Dahlonega, GA 30533
706-864-7777

GMD Computrack Atlanta/Motorcycle Pro Care (Repair Shop)
106 S Ave
Fairmount, GA 30139
(706) 337-4114

Motorcycle Trailers:

Cowboy Custom Trailers
1741 Blue Ridge Highway
Blairsville, Georgia 30512
706-835-2243

Motorcycle Apparel & Accessories:

The Rider's Outpost
98 Dean Goss Drive, Suite 108
Jasper, GA 30143
706-253-5122

Chattahoochee Biker Gear
8065 South Main St.
Helen, GA 30545
706-878-0076

Restaurants:

Walker's Fried Pies & BBQ
2183 Georgia 52 East
Ellijay, GA 30536
(706) 635-1223

Dairy Queen
1043 S Main St,
Ellijay, GA 30540
(706) 635-2020

El Rey Cantina
945 Maddox Dr
Ellijay, GA 30540
706-276-1515

Subway Restaurants (Numerous Locations – See Ad in Book)
Corporate Offices
772 Maddox Drive, Suite 138
East Ellijay, GA 30540
(706) 515-0013

Panorama Orchards & Farm Market
Hwy 515 South
63 Talona Spur
Ellijay, GA 30540
706-276-3813

Cajun Depot Grill
67 Depot Street Suite 101, Ellijay, GA 30540
706-276-1676

Campgrounds:

Wildcat Lodge and Campground
7475 Georgia Hwy 60
Suches, GA 30572
(706) 747-1011
GPS Coordinates - +34° 43' 11.52", -84° 4' 1.54"

Murphy / Peace Valley KOA Campground
117 Happy Valley Road
Marble, NC 28905
828-837-6223

Timberlake Campground
3270 Conleys Creek Road
Whittier, North Carolina 28789
828-497-7320

Motels:

Best Western of Murphy
1522 Andrews Road
Murphy, NC 28906
828-837-3060

Motorcycle Rentals & Tours:

Riders Hill
3003 Morrison Moore Parkway E.
Dahlonega, GA 30533
706-864-7777

Motorcycle Rentals & Tours:

Smoky Mountain Motorcycle Tours & Rentals
157 Poplar Hill Rd.
Stecoah, NC (Robbinsville Area) 28771
828.479.6600

General Shopping – Crafts & Home Accents:

Whistle Tree Pottery
10 North Main Street
Ellijay, GA 30540
706-698-1223

Southern Grace
40 River St., Suite A
Ellijay, GA 30540
706-515-1090
706-515-1093

Publications & Advertising:

Born To Ride Magazine Georgia Edition
6172 Duncan Bridge Road
Cleveland, GA 30528
(706) 865-4140

North Georgia Motorcycles / Appalachian Computer Services
1007 South Main St.
Ellijay, GA 30540
(706) 635-6870
www.northgeorgiamotorcycles.com

Eric Wieberg

AS ALWAYS,
RIDE SAFE AND RIDE OFTEN!

Eric Wieberg

Made in the USA
Charleston, SC
09 May 2013